# A Kid's Guide to Drawing America™

# How to Draw
# Maine's
# Sights and Symbols

Jenny Deinard

The Rosen Publishing Group's
PowerKids Press™
New York

*To Teddy*

Published in 2002 by The Rosen Publishing Group, Inc.
29 East 21st Street, New York, NY 10010

First Edition

Book Design: Kim Sonsky
Layout Design: Michael Donnellan
Project Editor: Jannell Khu

Illustration Credits: Jamie Grecco except p. 19 by Emily Muschinske.
Photo Credits: pp. 7, 16, 18, 24, 26 © Index Stock; p. 8 (sketch), p. 9 (painting) © 2001 Board of Trustees, National Gallery of Art, Washington; pp. 12, 14 © One Mile Up, Incorporated; p. 20 © Tim Zurowski/CORBIS; p. 22 © Jan Butchofsky-Houser/CORBIS; p. 28 courtesy of Maine Audio Visual Services.

Deinard, Jenny
How to draw Maine's sights and symbols /Jenny Deinard.
p.  cm. — (A kid's guide to drawing America)
Includes index.
Summary:  This book explains how to draw some of Maine's sights and symbols, including the state seal, the official flower, and the Harriet Beecher Stowe House.
  ISBN 0-8239-6075-7
1.  Emblems, State—Maine—Juvenile literature  2.  Maine—In art—Juvenile literature  3.  Drawing—Technique—Juvenile literature [1.  Emblems, State—Maine  2.  Maine 3.  Drawing—Technique] I. Title II.  Series
  2001
  743'.8'99741—dc21

Manufactured in the United States of America

# CONTENTS

# Let's Draw Maine

Maine has more than 3,500 miles (5,633 km) of coastline and more than 2,000 islands off its coast. With all of this water and coastline, seafood is one of Maine's major industries. In 1997, 47 million pounds (21.4 million kg) of lobster were harvested off Maine's shore! If you visit Maine, you might feast on clams, mussels, or freshly caught fish, as well as lobster. Afterwards you might relax on a beach, take a stroll through a pine forest, or even catch a glimpse of the official state animal, the moose! You might climb a mountain in Acadia National Park and watch the sun rise.

You also can eat blueberries in Maine. Maine produces 98 percent of all the blueberries grown in America. Maine is also one of the top three potato-producing states in the country.

Maine has a rich history that you can explore by learning more about its sights and symbols. With this book, you also can learn how to draw some of Maine's sights and symbols.  Here are some hints and tips to help you use this book. All of the drawings begin with a simple shape. From there you will add other shapes. Each new step of the drawing is shown in red to help guide you. You can check out the drawing terms below for help, too. Here are the supplies that you will need to draw the sights and symbols of Maine:

- A sketch pad
- An eraser
- A number 2 pencil
- A pencil sharpener

These are some of the shapes and drawing terms you need to know to draw Maine's sights and symbols:

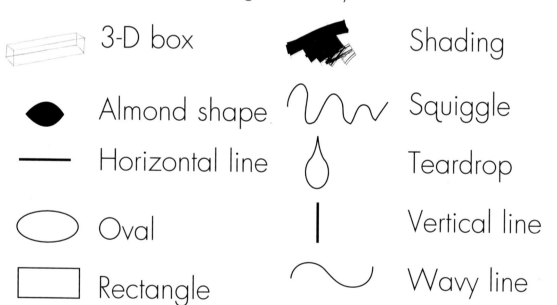

3-D box

Shading

Almond shape

Squiggle

Horizontal line

Teardrop

Oval

Vertical line

Rectangle

Wavy line

# The Pine Tree State

Maine has many nicknames. One nickname is the Pine Tree State, which celebrates Maine's 17 million acres (6.8 million ha) of forest that covers more than 90 percent of the state. Forests provide Maine with one of its important natural resources and industries. The state is called the Lumber State because of this industry. Maine is called the Border State because it borders the country of Canada. It also is called the Old Dirigo State because its motto is *dirigo*, which is Latin for "I lead" or "I direct." No one knows for certain where the name Maine came from. It is thought to have come from either the name of the French province Mayne, brought to America by French colonists, or from the word "main," as in "mainland." The coast of Maine is called Down East because ships traveling from Boston, Massachusetts, to towns along the coast of Maine sail with the wind behind them, or downwind, as they travel east. Maine covers 33,741 square miles (87,388 sq km) of land and has a population of 1,253,000 people.

You can find many pinecones in Maine. In fact, one of Maine's nicknames is the Pine Tree State.

# Artist in Maine

Winslow Homer

Winslow Homer is one of America's greatest watercolorists and realist painters. Realism is a school of art in which painters attempt to paint exactly what they see, paying careful attention to light and shadow. Homer was born in Boston, Massachusetts, in 1836. At the age of 19, he began work for the lithography firm. His illustrations caught the attention of *Harper's Weekly*, a popular magazine. *Harper's* sent Homer to draw images of the Civil War. He made oil paintings from some of these drawings, one of which, *Prisoners From the Front*, hangs in the Metropolitan Museum of Art in New York.

Homer captures the sea waves and the strong wind as it rocks the little boat in his sketch, *Breezing Up (A Fair Wind)*.

Homer spent 1881 and 1882 in a fishing village in England. When he returned to America, he settled permanently in Prout's Neck, Maine, and he died there in 1910. His time spent in England left a deep impression on Homer and inspired him to paint sea themes for the rest of his life. Homer used seascape backgrounds to capture the relationship between people and nature. Take a look at *Breezing Up (A Fair Wind)*. Although the sea wind is strong and the water currents are rough, the boys look relaxed and at home in the little sailboat. In fact, they almost look like they are part of the sea!

In 1876, Homer painted *Breezing Up (A Fair Wind)* in Maine. It was done in oil on canvas and measures 24 ³⁄₁₆" x 38 ³⁄₁₆" (61.4 cm x 97 cm).

# Map of Maine

Map of the Continental United States

Maine is located in the northeastern corner of the United States and borders New Hampshire. It is the only state that borders only one other state. The rest of Maine borders the Atlantic Ocean and Canada. The state's highest point is Mount Katahdin, which is 5,268 feet (1,606 m) above sea level. Maine has 12 major ski areas and 436,064 acres (176,469 ha) of state and national parks. The only national park in New England, Acadia National Park, is in Maine. The park covers more than 47,000 acres (19,020 ha) of land. If you visit Acadia National Park, make sure to see Cadillac Mountain. From October 7 to March 6, Cadillac Mountain is the first place in the United States from which to see the sun rise!

**1**

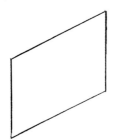

Start your map of Maine by drawing a slanted rectangle.

**2**

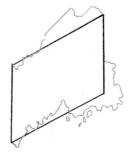

Use the rectangle as a guide and add details to the shape of Maine.

**3**

Erase extra lines and draw a circle to mark Fort Knox.

**4**

Draw in the Harriet Beecher Stowe House by using a square with an open triangle on top.

**5**

Use a rounded rectangle to mark a Maine lighthouse.

**6**

Use a triangle and a small rectangle to mark Baxter State Park.

**7**

Draw a star to mark Maine's capital city, Augusta.

**8**

| | |
|---|---|
| ☆ | Augusta |
| ○ | Fort Knox |
| ⌂ | Harriet Beecher Stowe House |
| ▯ | Maine lighthouse |
| ⌂ | Baxter State Park |

Use the key box to make sure you drew in all of Maine's points of interest.

# The State Seal

Maine's state seal was adopted in 1820, the year that Maine became a state. There is an image of the state animal, the moose, on a silver shield. Behind the moose is a pine tree to represent Maine's great forests. On the right side of the shield is a sailor. He stands for the importance of the sea to Maine's economy. To the left of the shield is a farmer. He represents agriculture in Maine. He holds a scythe, a tool that cuts grain and grass. The men stand on a blue banner that reads "Maine." The red banner above them reads "*Dirigo,*" the state's motto, which means "I direct" or "I lead" in Latin. The star above the red banner represents the North Star, the star that sailors and fishermen use to lead them north.

**1**

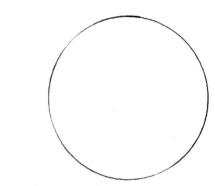

Draw a large circle.

**2**

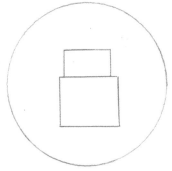

Then add two rectangles for the shield.

**3**

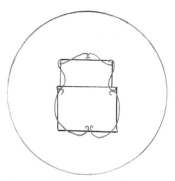

Draw the shape of the shield using the rectangles as guides.

**4**

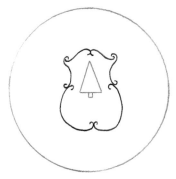

Erase extra lines and add a triangle and a rectangle for the tree.

**5**

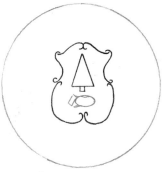

Add two rectangles and an oval for the moose.

**6**

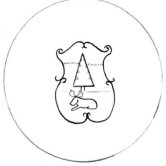

Draw in the moose's horns and body, erase extra lines, and add a wavy line for the tree line.

**7**

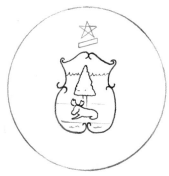

Draw the star, banner, and grass.

**8**

Write the word "MAINE" in the lower banner. Add the finishing details and shade the seal.

# The State Flag

Maine became a state on March 15, 1820. It was the twenty-third state to join the Union. The first state flag of Maine was flown from 1901 to 1909. This flag simply showed a green pine tree and a blue star in the center of a pale yellow background. Maine's current state flag was adopted in 1909. It is similar in design to the flag carried by Maine's armed forces during the Civil War. The background of the flag is military blue, which is the same blue that is used in the U.S. flag. An image of the state seal is centered on the flag.

**1**

To draw Maine's flag, draw a large rectangle for the flag's field. Add two small ovals for the men's heads.

**2**

Then add two rectangles for bodies.

**3**

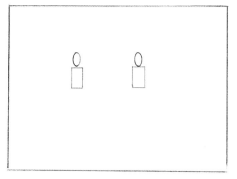

For the legs, draw four thin rectangles underneath the men's bodies.

**4**

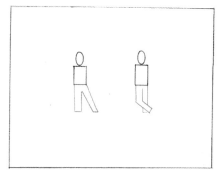

Add the men's arms. Notice how the shapes of the arms are bent.

**5**

Add details to the men and add an anchor and a scythe. Erase extra lines.

**6**

Then add a curved rectangle as a banner. Now add the North Star.

**7**

To draw the center part of the flag, refer to the Maine state seal.

**8**

Add detail and shading, and write the word "MAINE." Your flag is done!

# The White Pine

The white pine (*Pinus strobus*) became the official tree of Maine in 1945. It also is known as the eastern white pine, the spruce pine, and the northern white pine. It is thought to be the largest conifer in the northeastern United States. The bark of the white pine is purplish gray with deep ridges. The needles are bluish green to silver-green. Because of its ability to resist decay and termites, the white pine is a popular material used to build ships. North American white pines were used to make the famous British navy ships of the eighteenth and nineteenth centuries. There used to be many more white pines throughout northeastern America, but they were nearly wiped out by the timber industry and by a tree fungus known as blister rust.

**1**

Start the pine tree by drawing a long, thin triangle.

**2**

Then add a wider triangle over the first one you just drew.

**3**

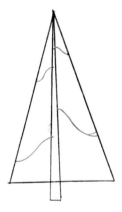

Start drawing in branches using wavy lines.

**4**

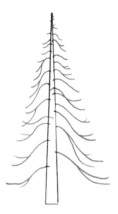

Finish all the branches and erase the larger triangle.

**5**

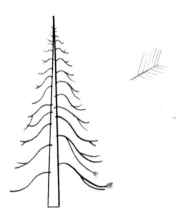

Draw the pine needles with short, straight lines on each branch. The more needles you draw, the fuller the tree will look.

**6**

Add shading and detail, and you're done!

# The White Pine Cone and Tassel

The white pine cone (*Pinus strobus Linnaeus*) and tassel became Maine's official state flower in 1895. It does not have the colorful, soft petals or the sweet smell of a flower, but the hard pinecone is indeed the flower of the American white pine tree. It is a strobilus, which is a kind of fruit or bloom that is cone-shaped, with thin, rounded scales that overlap. The head of a wheat stalk is another example of a strobilus. White pine cones are 4–8 inches (10–20 cm) long and are a yellowish brown color. The cones have a sticky, fragrant substance called resin. Pine resin has been used for hundreds of years for a variety of purposes. People have used resin to make soap, turpentine, and rosin, which is used to soften violin bows.

1

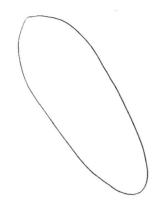

Start by drawing a long oval. Notice that the cone is a bit wider at the top.

2

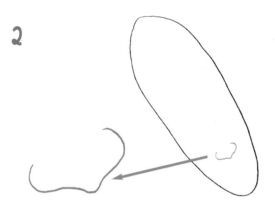

Practice drawing the shape of the seeds. The shape looks like the bottom of a nose. Pinecones have many of these seeds. They are layered like shingles on a roof.

3

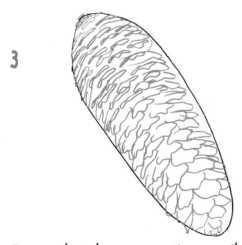

Repeat that shape many times until you fill the oval with rows of seeds. Look at the photograph and notice that toward the top of the cone the seeds are packed close together. Their shape appears to be thinner.

4

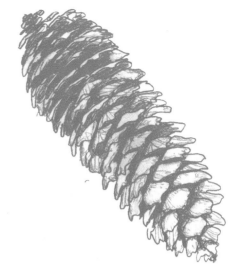

Erase the oval guide. Shade the pinecone. Notice that the pinecone is darkest underneath each seed.

19

# The Black-Capped Chickadee

The black-capped chickadee became Maine's state bird in 1927. It is named for its black head and for its song, which sounds like "chika-dee-dee-dee." A chickadee is a kind of bird called a titmouse. The word titmouse comes from the Old Icelandic word *titr*, which means "something small" and the Old English word *mase*, which means "small bird." This is a good way to describe the chickadee, which is only about 5 inches (13 cm) long.

The chickadee is known for being so tame that it will perch on the end of a human finger and will learn simple tricks. The chickadee has special muscles in its legs that help it swing upside down from the tips of branches while it chases insects!

**1**

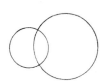

Draw two circles for the bird's head and body. Notice that the circles overlap.

**2**

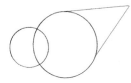

Now add a triangle. This will be the bird's lower body and tail.

**3**

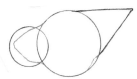

Connect the triangle and circles to form the shape of the bird.

**4**

Erase extra lines. Your bird should resemble the above drawing.

**5**

Use three triangles to draw the bird's beak, wing, and tail. Notice that the triangles are all different sizes.

**6**

Add detail to the bird's wing. Add a small rectangle for the top of the bird's leg.

**7**

Soften the bird's wings. Draw a line in the bird's tail. Use thin lines for the bird's feet. Add two thin rectangles for the branch.

**8**

Draw a small circle for the bird's eye. Add detail and shading to the bird and you're done!

21

# Maine's Lighthouses

There are 68 lighthouses along Maine's 3,500 miles (5,633 km) of coastline. Lighthouses were built to warn ships and boats of rocky coastlines and to prevent them from running aground.

At a height of 133 feet (41 m), the Boon Island Light is the tallest lighthouse in Maine. If you visit this lighthouse, be prepared to climb 130 steps to the light at the top! The Portland Head Light, in Cape Elizabeth, is Maine's oldest lighthouse. Its light first shone on January 1, 1791. The Sequin Light, in Georgetown, is the state's most powerful lighthouse. Its light can be seen for 26 miles (42 km). The lens over the light was installed in 1857, and it still works!

1

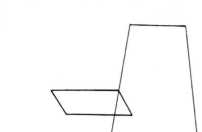

Draw two slanted rectangles.

2

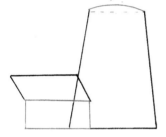

Round off the top of the larger rectangle. Add another rectangle to the smaller rectangle. This is the side part of the building.

3

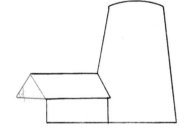

Erase extra lines and add a small triangle for the top front part of the smaller building.

4

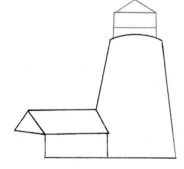

Add two rectangles and a triangle to the top of the lighthouse.

5

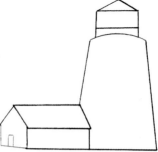

Finish the house with two short lines and add a rectangle for the door. Erase extra lines.

6

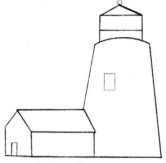

Use a rectangle for the lighthouse window and add a circle on top the roof.

7

Round off all the lines on top of the lighthouse and add a curved line for the ground.

8

Erase extra lines. Add as much detail and shading as you'd like, and your lighthouse is done.

# The Harriet Beecher Stowe House

Harriet Beecher Stowe wrote *Uncle Tom's Cabin*, the most famous antislavery literature in American history. Many people believe this novel started the Civil War. Stowe was born in Connecticut, on June 14, 1811. In 1832, she moved to Ohio, to teach. Ohio borders Kentucky, one of the southern states that practiced slavery. This is where Stowe saw slavery firsthand. In 1850, Stowe moved into a house at 63 Federal Street in Brunswick, Maine, where she wrote her famous book. Today, this house is called the Harriet Beecher Stowe House and it is used as an inn. Although Stowe died on July 1, 1896, she lives on through her book, which has become a classic and was translated into 23 languages!

1

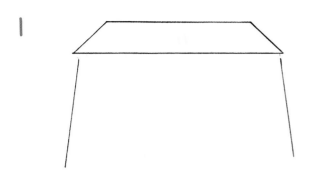

Draw a large, slanted rectangle for the shape of the roof, and two slanted lines for the sides of the building.

2

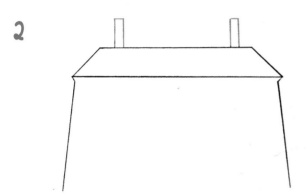

Add two small rectangles on top of the roof for the chimneys.

3

Use slanted rectangles to draw the windows. This slant will make it seem as though you are looking up at the building.

4

Connect the bottom of the house with a long line. Now add a slanted rectangle for the door.

5

Draw two rectangles for the fence posts, and divide each window into three parts.

6

Add shading and detail to the house, like the chimney bricks, the window shutters, the house door, the entrance steps, and the fence bars. Nice job!

# The Moose

The moose, which got its name from the Algonquian Native American word *mus*, was adopted as Maine's official state animal in 1979. Male moose, or bulls, can stand more than 6 feet (2 m) tall and can weigh more than 1,400 pounds (635 kg). To drink from a shallow pool of water, moose have to kneel! Bulls have huge bone growths on their heads, called antlers. These antlers can have up to 30 spikes and can grow more than 5 feet (2 m) wide. Adult bulls shed their antlers once a year, in November or December, and they grow new antlers. Moose fur varies from light brown to almost black. Their hind legs are shorter than their forelegs. This makes them look hunchbacked. Moose often are seen alone but gather in groups in the winter.

**1**

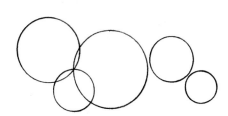

To start, draw five circles. Notice that the circles are different sizes and some overlap.

**2**

Now connect the five circles to create the outline of the moose.

**3**

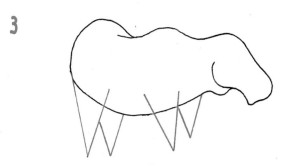

Erase extra lines and add four triangles for legs.

**4**

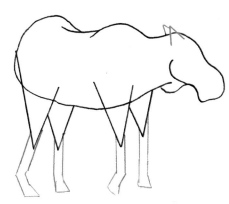

Finish the legs with thin rectangles. For the ears, add two small triangles on top of the head.

**5**

Soften the ears with curves. Erase extra lines. Now add an eye. Draw the shape of the antlers. Notice that they are curved and wavy on top.

**6**

Add shading and you're done.

# Maine's Capitol

Maine's state house is in Augusta, the state capital. It sits on 34 acres (14 ha) near the Kennebec River. Architect Charles Bulfinch, who also designed the Massachusetts state house, designed the building. The first Maine legislature met in the state house on January 4, 1832. The cornerstone for the state house was laid on July 4, 1829. The building took three years to complete. It is about 150 feet (46 m) long with two wings that extend north and south. The center section has columns and a cupola, a popular decoration of the federal style. A dome later replaced the original cupola. On top of the dome is a statue that represents wisdom. It is made of copper and covered with gold.

**1**

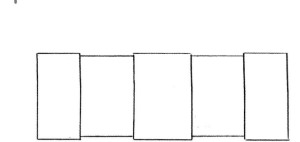

Draw five rectangles. Notice that the second and the fourth rectangles are slightly smaller than the other three rectangles.

**2**

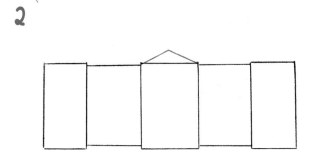

Add a triangle on top of the center rectangle.

**3**

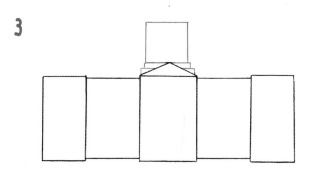

Draw two thin rectangles and a larger one for the base of the dome.

**4**

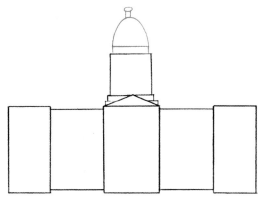

Draw a small rectangle on top of the last shape you drew. Add a half oval. Now draw a thin rectangle and a small oval on top of that shape.

**5**

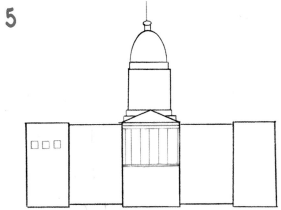

To finish the dome, draw a straight line for the pole. Now add long rectangles for the columns and small squares for the windows.

**6**

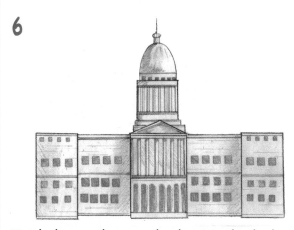

Finish the windows and columns. Shade the building. Shade with more pressure for the windows to make them darker. Erase any smudges.

29

# Maine State Facts

| | |
|---|---|
| Statehood | March 15, 1820, 23rd state |
| Area | 33,741 sq miles (87,388 sq km) |
| Population | 1,253,000 |
| Capital | Augusta, population, 20,400 |
| Most Populated City | Portland, population, 63,100 |
| Industries | Health services, tourism, forest products, food processing, leather products |
| Agriculture | Seafood, potatoes, eggs, and poultry |
| Tree | White pine |
| Nickname | Pine Tree State |
| State Song | "State of Maine Song" |
| State Motto | *Dirigo*, I direct |
| Bird | Black-capped chickadee |
| Flower | White pine cone and tassel |
| Cat | Maine coon cat |
| Fossil | *Pertica quadrifaria* |
| Mineral | Tourmaline |
| Fish | Landlocked salmon |
| Animal | Moose |
| Insect | Honeybee |
| Berry | Wild blueberry |
| State Vessel | Schooner *Bowdoin* |

# Glossary

**conifer** (KA-nih-fur)  An evergreen tree that bears cones, such as pine, spruce, or fir.

**cornerstone** (KOR-nur-stohn)  The first, usually large, stone placed when constructing a building.

**cupola** (KYOO-puh-luh)  A small structure built on a roof.

**economy** (ih-KAH-nuh-mee)  The way a country or business manages its resources.

**industries** (IN-dus-treez)  Systems of work, or labor.

**lithography** (lih-THAH-gruh-fee)  A type of printing process in which an image is imprinted on a smooth surface.

**perch** (PURCH)  A place where something sits or is hung.

**population** (pah-pyoo-LAY-shun)  The number of people who live in a region.

**province** (PRAH-vints)  A country, area, or place.

**resin** (REH-zin)  A sticky liquid that some trees release to cover holes in their bark.

**running aground** (RUHN-ing uh-GROWND)  When a boat hits the bottom and becomes stuck.

**scythe** (SYTH)  A tool with a long, curved blade, which is used for cutting grass or crops.

**translated** (TRANS-layt-ed)  To have taken words from one language and turned them into another.

**turpentine** (TUR-pen-tyn)  A liquid that is mixed with paints and other substances to make them thinner.

# Index

# Web Sites

For more information on Maine check out this Web site:
www.state.me.us